T0131651

A Poet's Journey Continued

More Faith, Humor, and Reflections

RICHARD A. CARDNER

WESTBOW
PRESS®
A DIVISION OF THOMAS NELSON
& ZONDERVAN

WestBow Press books may be ordered through booksellers or by contacting:

WestBow Press
A Division of Thomas Nelson & Zondervan
1663 Liberty Drive
Bloomington, IN 47403
www.westbowpress.com
844-714-3454

Scripture quotations taken from The Holy Bible, New International
Version® NIV® Copyright © 1973 1978 1984 2011 by Biblica, Inc.
TM. Used by permission. All rights reserved worldwide.

Some poems are based on biblical accounts found in
the NIV Life Application Study Bible 2011.

ISBN: 978-1-6642-9085-3 (sc)
ISBN: 978-1-6642-9084-6 (hc)
ISBN: 978-1-6642-9086-0 (e)

Library of Congress Control Number: 2023901590

Print information available on the last page.

WestBow Press rev. date: 3/15/2023

To the love of my life,
my wife, Linda

Contents

Preface

One day as I was sitting at my computer, I noticed something: the desktop was a mess. I decided to use the pandemic isolation to solve the neatness problem, and doing so allowed me to finalize some poems and gather them together in this book.

Several people and groups have influenced my work. I'll name a few, but don't blame them. First, my wife did yeoman labor in editing. This is a blessing, as I am not a patient person.

Second, I have belonged to numerous writing groups over the years, including the NH Poetry Society and several groups in Arizona. Each group has helped by reviewing my work and by suggesting prompts to jump start the writing.

November 2021

At Sixes and Sevens

I drove slowly on through the oily-smelling night fog.
Old landmarks, once bright, were smudged and smeared
as if they were being erased,
canceled out of the picture,

never again to lighten a life.
People carrying six-foot poles walked slightly stooped.
Each pinprick of mist
added to their load.

It looked like my hometown,
but this world was slightly off-kilter.
Inverted stoplights did not bode well,
and the healthy were called ill.

Ahead I saw a dull glow
where I recalled a strip mall, Peaceful Stop,
but now named on the flickering neon sign
PIECEMEA with a hanging L.

The hardware store had only soft goods.
Tired people did not rest at the restaurant.
Guarded pails of money sat outside the laundromat.
Disheveled children wandered

aimlessly

in front of the boarded-up childcare center.

My body was not in sync;
my mind, drained of fine words.
My good sleep slept.

But I was startled awake from fruitless slumber to the
enshrouded hill-mounted cross still brightly
glowing in this miasmic world.

October 24, 2020

A Ball at the Mall

Young Mother Ball
went to the mall
to buy herself some stuff.

Getting to it
with a full wallet
still never was enough.

September 24, 2006

Beginnings

Before beginnings,
in the darkness no thing reigned:
no thing to have form
before the light was seated;
no time to have a before.

March 6, 2014

The Boat

He rowed the boat toward the depths
with deeply dipped oars.

The sweat dripped from each pore,
his shirt no longer dry.

As soon as the deeps were reached,
he lifted the oars.

The cloud-clotted sky shouted
as a friend warns one.

He smiled at the wind's harsh drive,
at its cooling blow,
at its boat-breaching waves,

and turned the boat to face the threat.

April 8, 2013

The Boundary

When he reflected on his life,
but before he stood at the edge,
he saw that he wanted
for nothing.
Any need or even desire
was met and soon in his grasp.
He had filled himself and
lacked no thing.

Yet
as he focuses beyond the edge
that's between his now-known desert past
and the promised, fogged-in land,
something gnaws and draws him.
Then he knows he must not wander back
but step over that jagged border—
or forever wonder
"Do I have every thing?"

January 8, 2014

The Boy, the Boat, and the Grandfather

On a late June day,
with sun-warmed arms I ran to
the dock-secured boat.
I checked the engine fuel tank;
petrol smell stung my young lungs.

The oars were in place
in our flat-bottomed rowboat
built by my uncle.
(I didn't plan on oars, but
I wear belts and suspenders.)

A tug on the rope,
and the engine vroomed to life.
I steered past the raft
along the stone-faced earth dam
my great-grandfather helped build.

In a quarter mile,
if five horses would let me,
I chose to showboat;
looking ahead for danger,
I pushed the throttle forward.

Right, then back—no fright.
In ever sharper angles,
I forced the short boat.
On one turn, the stern lifted;
off came the engine—*kerplunk.*

It sank down, dankly down.
I boyed, not manned, the big oars
to the mishap site.
There, in ten feet of water,
were both my engine and heart.

Not wanting to dive,
I rowed slowly to the dam
and tree-tied the boat
in line with the engine's grave.
I walked, head down, back to camp.

Grandfather listened to my woeful tale
and thought … and thought more.
He brought out a burlap sack
and carried it to the moored boat,
then rowed to the site.

His bag held iceman's tongs
whose handles he'd roped.
Would hope-pulled handles close the
ancient ice tongs' pincer bite?

We lowered the tongs;
The engine's U-shaped handle
was missed. Lousy luck.
Again.
Success!

We pulled the engine
into the boat, and I sighed.
My day was not done.
I usually looked forward to
greeting my father's return.

Today is diff'rent.
I must explain what happened.
No storm rose; in fact,
in sun I had to fix what
I had done, and that was that.

January 23, 2016

Breeze

You know those Arizona days
of still, dead oven heat,
when a deep, dry breath scorches
and diaphanous mirages are shimmering sheets.

When I think I can take no more,
this makes me feel unwell:
A slight breeze enlivens leaves.
I ask, "Where do breezes dwell?"

In mountainous crannies and crooks?
Or the intestines of a cave?
Or spun off in a hurricane wake
and skipped from wave to wave?

Do they dwell in waving prairie grass
or slide down glacial slope?
No matter! I ponder too much;
wherever they are is hope.

October 10, 2020

The Call

Some hear the call
and run to answer
directly into battle.
Others seek a test
to allay their doubt
or remove the cloud.

For them, it is in such a cloud
that they do not hear the call.
This adds to their doubt
of their ability to answer,
worried they'll fail the test
and lose the battle.

Gideon was one such worrier of battle.
To remove the cloud,
he asked for a sign
to prove the call
so he might answer
and resolve his doubt.

He asked God to end doubt
and ensure victory in battle,
to give him the answer
that it was really God
and uncloud
his vision of the call.

Moses, unsure of his test,
tried God with his doubt.
Though he heard the call,
he wondered who he was
to convince his tribe to do battle,
to convince them it was God in the cloud
and that He had the answer.

Jonah did not answer
and left in a boat for Tarshish,
when up came a storm cloud.
Jonah ended in the belly of a fish, ending his doubt.
Soon he left for Nineveh to do battle
and still reluctantly answered the call.

All had their strength clouded and doubted,
but all also answered the test,
winning the battle to answer the call.

Judges 6:33–40; 7:4–8;
Exodus 3; book of Jonah

Contentment

He never left his home state for fun.
Except for his Canadian fishing,
for other sites he had no wishing,
Content to live the small-town life,
which with his relatives was rife.
To me, a child, it was my gain
to know him in sun or rain.

He was skilled of hand and with a gun.
He made a wagon all of wood
that I but once down driveway pulled,
returned to him with child's complaint,
"This is no good for me, a saint."
I saw only me, as was my part,
and missed the sliver in his heart.

June 11, 2008

The Cross

The metal cross slides across the surface,
then slowly moves like a pendulum
as it makes a crescent, right to left, left to right,
sinking deeper on each swing.

A fish nips at the cross,
briefly mouths then spits it out.
A plume of sea sand drifts up
as the cross slowly settles on the bottom.
… … … … … … …
Over centuries the metal's encrusted;
currents repeatedly cover and uncover it.

Fluffy clouds float; a swimmer dives.
He sees the cross-shaped form and scoops it up.
Back at his boat, he bags the cross;
without haggling, he sells it to a curio shop.

The owner cleans the cross; silver glints
from behind the ocean's damage.
Customers glance, a few touch,
and all think the cross costs too much.
It remains unbought.

A new owner cleans out the shop;
he gives the unsought cross
to a fidgety unsmiling child,
who rubs it as he goes home.

He plays with it, removing layers of grime,
and quickly gasps when
his effort to polish the silver reveals gold
And births a smile.

He cradles the cross in his hands,
moves over to the window soon,
and slowly turns the cross in the sun.
The sun's rays warm him and light the room.

He crosses to his memento shelf,
clears it of past treasures, then fidgeting no more,
smiles as he sets his find on the shelf:

the sea's scarring accretions,
the silver,
the gold,
the cross.

June 19, 2017

Dawn

The pastel dawn grows
slowly, steadily broader,
mastering the night.

October 12, 2016

Disguises

You come in many guises,
but I always know it's you.
You cannot really disguise,
no matter what form you choose.

You are raised up with praises
for being sharp yet soft.
Your shape changes with your whim;
your perfume through air wafts.

Your beauty is such that
people nearby are improved.
You fit in varied decors.
Being lovely, you're thereby loved.

You're placed on a pedestal
to better receive homage.
When you enter a room we hear,
"Bravo! Pour le fromage."

February 25, 2012

Disintegration

In their disintegration,
dandelions build a nation.

April 10, 2020

Ease

I
find
this
prompt
hard.
Had
I
thought
more
to
please,
I
would
look
for
more
ease.

July 2, 2014

Empty

He took my empty field
and its nothing meaning.

He left ripening fruit which,
if eaten by the world and drunk,
would leave rest in its wake.

January 1, 2013

The Engagement

In his ardor, he proposed marriage and was accepted. He determined to make his sweetheart a hope chest, but being unskilled he asked his grandfather for help. They bought the materials from a Tennessee company. He lied to his fiancée as to why he could not be with her on Saturday mornings, scratching and scouring the engagement. Then he went to his grandfather's shop with its cedar smell and worked on the chest.

Near the end of the project, as he was fastening some knobs on the front of the chest, he slipped with a screwdriver and made a large gouge in the cedar. He gasped, but his grandfather, as usual, caught and taught him. The old man mixed the cedar sawdust with glue and filled in the damage. When the young man gave his love the chest, the Saturday morning scars were healed, just as the chest had been smoothed. Neither wound is visible today, forty-eight years later; the smell of the cedar lingers.

December 18, 2014

Exclamation Point!

As a sentence,
I am punctured
by punctuation.

I like the (.)
that lets me rest.

The (,) and
the (;)
give pause
before links.

The (?)
makes me think.

But the (!)'s
an emphatic horror.

Can I change my mind no more?

May 21, 2012

Faithfulness

Tanka for Ruth from the Book of Ruth

Six feet raised the dust.
Three voices wept in farewell.
One turned back to home.

Faithful Ruth with Naomi
went on to Naomi's town.

Family Ballad

The family clan gathers now
at ocean shore
again to build and relate
the family's treasured lore:

of people passed long ago,
of people now here present,
to create at this date
memories quite pleasant.

Within the bounds of this compound,
we spread out to the sea
with treasure hunts and spy camps
and food and fun and glee.
The elders sit around and tell
the oft-told tales of life—
some sad, some funny, some silly, some epic—
that speak of events and strife.

It amazes me to tell you now
how tightly these gatherings tie;
with each successive year's visit
it binds the family's lives.

June 22, 2013

Fire

I climb up the steep slope,
gasp in the heavy smoke
that rises from the fire.

My eyes water
to clear the soot.
My legs ache.

The brambles cut my hands,
which try for a hold
on the land.

The land levels out.
The smoke thins out.
The soot settles out.

I look back and see cars
with the soon-to-be homeless
as they leave houses.

The tearing starts again,
but this time the soot
is what I have in me.

I know the homeless heart.
I know the hunger pains.
I know the cold restless sleep

that moved me to throw
more tinder on the fire,
careless of its spread.

The tears now come in sobs,
muddying my dirty shirt
and the hard ground.

You ask, "What is the resolution?
Really, poet? Get real!
Maybe tomorrow."

March 10, 2014

Fresh Start

The prompt: use the phrase "fresh start" and start writing.

I need a fresh start on my writing.
So how can I think about this part?
Maybe I won't get it because I am an upstart.
No, that doesn't make sense, so my fresh start needs a new start.
Perhaps if I get up early, it will give me a head start.
What if I back up a bit for a restart?
Do I have the heart?
What do I wish to impart?
That looks good, but upon reflection it looks like a false start.
I know, I'll go to my writing group for a jump-start.
That should be at least a quick start.
Perhaps some of these ideas will give my writing a kick-start before
   I depart.
Well, this prompt is a start.

January 20, 2017

The Garden

He gardened grudges;
he hoed his hate
and wondered why
he lost his mate.

Then came the Word
spread in his life.
Nurtured by the Word
he found his wife.

September 7, 2020

Geese

I wandered around the park's man-made lake.
The fountain flowed hourly that afternoon,
white against the blue New Mexico sky.

I slowly walked up a slight slope.
I saw ahead a gaggle of geese;
they fed on the grass and, I guessed, seeds.

That's not all: they were in a bottle shape—
not a beer bottle nor a Coke bottle,
not a baby bottle but a bulbous shape.

It seemed strange, with such a large smorgasbord,
that all but a few would frequent this space.
Was it somehow the food? Their family?

I did not know, nor know now, geese's ways.
Soon it occurred to me that they, like I,
sought the shade of the tree in which to eat.

May 21, 2013

Giving Thanks

Idea from the Psalms

Bill's sideboard was full.
The prayer was said,
thanking God for the meal
of meat, sweets, and bread.

Phil's sideboard's not rife.
His prayer was felt,
thanking God for his life,
still in the Son's light.

November 28, 2006

Grow

Verses grow in good soil,
spine up and limbs sunward.
Foundation roots seek water for
treed words.

November 6, 2013

Home

I wait for the pitch.
It's a fast, low one.
My bunt slides away
spinning but in play.

The third baseman's slow.
He heads down the line,
one-hands it, wings it
past the first baseman's mitt.

The ball rolls to the fence;
I dig for second.
The next throw is wide,
on the outfield side,

so I head for third.
The coach signals stop,
But the fielder's arm's weak.
I go for glory's sake.

Fans shout as the ball
skitters to the shortstop.
On home plate I bow and
tip my hat to the crowd

for *my* home run.

December 18, 2014

Ice Cream

Poetry that obfuscates
I do not denigrate.
Words that are antiquated
I eagerly anticipate.

Meanings that we find abstruse
have their effective use.
Ice cream in a cruse
in my life deserves no abuse.

February 27, 2013

Ice-Skating Class

Prompted by the illustration Ice-Skating Class for Dad
by George Hughes, Saturday Evening Post, *February 8, 1858[1]*

A man was skating on ice.
His kids were very nice:
they helped him stay up
'til called home to sup,
leaving him flat, to be precise.

[1] This illustration was the subject of the *Saturday Evening Post*'s limerick contest, November/December 2015, http://www.saturdayeveningpost.com/limerick-contest#sthash.5zlWSE0Y.dpuf.

It's Everywhere

I leave the house in the chilly predawn;
the unseen sun's muted light diffused
as though seen through a lampshade.

Stonehenge Road was steep but I am fresh;
as I crest the top, the now unshaded sunlight
hits me straight on; makes me weep.

I came near the nursery swamp
that nurtured new life while
damply filtering our wastes.

I pass a school,
descend to cross Frost's waywardly cool west-running brook
and tip my hat to his farm.

Then down, steeply down, to Ezekiel's Pond,
home to the native who saved hungry settlers,
pointing them to the Merrimack's eels beyond the tree.

Near the Rainbow School,
I detour along the rail trail
that knifes through a dark wood's glow.

The level surface made for ancient engines
welcomes my tired engine
after the previous hours of hills
and dales.

I stumbled in the shaded erosions;
I made my way to the pond's edge,
                    marveling that my walking stick
                              "bent" in the water.

I open and light a can of Sterno;
its blue and orange flame
                    flickers and heats my tea.

I drink, eat my sandwich and
wonder if Ezekiel wondered, as he ate,
what the light-skinned people would bring.

Back on the road I arrive at
the stop … wait … go lights at the five-road intersection which
makes the crossing safer.

I reach the garden center
just as the sun slides.

The pine-filtered light surrenders to
stars. Those stellar witnesses to billions of years
slowly twinkle into view, salting the heavens,
                    flashing to others
                              their ancient mating light's

                    whisper.

June 15, 2016

The Junkyard

The junkyard is full of old cars
and spilt chemicals,
once proud when well combined
before their fall.

My mission: to make a car that I and others can ride upon.

But how to start?

Get parts and cobble them together?

But what works for me might not for others.
I might be short or strong or nearsighted,
and they not.

This is an impossible task: this reconstruction
and re-creation of motion for many
from parts once serviceable but now dispersed.

So I get unmatched wheels, a frame, some brakes, the engine and
a steering wheel.

I am happy to stand while driving but others
might need to sit, so seats are settled.

Outside the fence were those who would ride;
they'll deride my sorrowful carriage.

And I fret too much their words:

I'm limited; alone, the world is too large.

So I'll build a mismatched car
fit for the me God created.

Those who can will ride;
perchance other cars from this vale of bones
will be resurrected.

October 2005

Knock

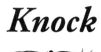

"Get down from there, you clown," she said.

Thus his song was knocked to its end
for too much chatter at a song site.

Years went by, then at a glee club
he took and passed the first test cut.

The prof heard try two and said,
"If I'd more time, I could train you."

Nice knockdown.

Still, he liked to sing, though he knew
of his short range, tin tone, brief breath.

He sought to vent his love,
so he went to his last hope place.

There they would, would they not, take him
if he could make a noise joy filled?

He went to the oak-crossed church door
and found it open at his knock.

There their love and his joy-filled noise
would melt any dry old clown-scold heart.

September 20, 2012

Leaving

We tromped up the hill.
Breeze blew fall leaves round our feet;
our steps flattened them.

The kaleidoscope
of colors fell around us,
too many to count.

The usual ones—
red, orange, yellow, mottled—
predominated.

The other colors—
sangria, seaweed, mocha—
added to our day.

We stooped to capture
a few of these hued floaters.
We learn by our touch:

one's like a nail file;
one more soft and leathery;
one crinkly and crisp.

We looked up to see
how they separately fell,
each in its own way.

One fell like a spear,
stem down, nearly impaling
the road beneath.

Some as concave boats
drifted back-forth, pendulum-like,
settling on sea road.

Some defiantly
clung to their twig, resisting
their ultimate fall.

Others leisurely,
gracefully drift as if on
a spiral staircase.

We sauntered back down,
strolling through piles of leaves to
our fire-warmed cottage.

October 15, 2019

Level

It's level at the cross's base
where our Savior died,
so all who seek at that same place
safely may abide.

January 19, 2018

Life Is ...

I snapped my pencil; I paced and could not stay still. *Oh man, what a struggle!*

At first it seemed it would be easy; wouldn't three score and ten years bring with them many ideas? Nope. Everywhere I went I came upon cliché after cliché: "Life is a bowl of cherries" and "This wonderful life."

Would not my many years of adventures bring a freshet of ideas to sate my appetite? No way. Nothing clever, no thing full of insights.

Stalled, stymied, and stuck.

(No, don't look at the last phrase as The Answer.)

Fancies did not fly to me; they did not dance near or far, as far as I could see.

I thought thoughts and oughts but all for naught. (I could say none were caught, but that addition would be fraught with readers who fought the overreaching rhymes.)

So at this point I have distilled my lessons down to this:

"Life is ..."

TO BE CONTINUED

Love and Fear

There is a certain phrase,
and when it's thought about,
it makes me want to smile,
to dance, to sing, to shout.

There are two emotions;
of conflict, there's no doubt.
But in their epic struggle,
Perfect Love drives fear out.

September 6, 2020
Inspired by a PBS show on folk music and by 1 John 4:18

Mall

When first I went to the mall,
I thought, *It'll be a dance.*
Not just any dance, a ball—
when first I went to the mall.
But there I saw no waltz at all,
and I took not a leaving glance
when first I went to the mall
and thought, *It'll be a dance.*

November 30, 2009

The Mission

We thought if we let our enemy know
what they were doing to us,
surely they would turn
from our rank slaughter.

Wouldn't they?

We sent our best on a dank mission,
knowing they would not return.

But

in a wretchedly slow way, it worked.
Our enemy's more sensitive ones retched.
Their laws pushed toward genocide's end and
their pile of our bloody tusks shrank.

Mother Wesley

On the mother of a Methodist founder

A weary Mother Wesley
takes her floor-length apron,
raises its hem over her head,
retreats into the twilight,
where no one bothers her.

A calmer Mother Wesley
folds her hands upon her lap
with no hemming or hawing,
advances into that light
where nothing bothers her.

March 3, 2010

Naught

I'm having trouble
with this prompt,
finding the middle thought.

You'd think I'd get it
right away,
looking for my light.

The more I think,
the more I fret—
it gives me such a fright

to see the prompt
that I'd suggested
coming to naught.

January 14, 2011

Octavia

Octavia watched from behind the glass
as a solitary tear slid down her face.
The children rode their little bikes,
but she was not allowed a place.

Enough of this, she sniffed and thought.
If I can walk, then I can ride.
Her large head, which prompted jeers,
would now not be a thing to hide.

She made her way to the garage,
opened it, and crossed the floor
to the unused bike against the wall—
she thought the thing would love to soar.

She wrapped her arms around the bar,
pushed the bike to the sloping road,
put one leg on a pedal
while the other balanced the load.

She gave a little push and coasted
slowly down the vacant street;
she started to work the pedals
then braked where the two roads meet.

The bike began to wobble and weave,
and when she tried to correct the course,
she got caught in the spokes and over she went,
roughly dumped with considerable force.

With only minor bruises, she smiled:
I can do this now; don't hesitate!
Others have just four feeble limbs,
and I have, count 'em, eight.

February 20, 2017

The Office

The corner room was small,
with one normal window;
the other, slightly higher
so only sky and treetops were seen.

The office was awfully cluttered.
He tried to clean it once in a while,
but the effort was doomed—
not under a cosmic curse, but by poor habits.

The books were Dewey-decimalized,
but items brought in were dropped

in the hurry to more urgent things.

One cloud in his sky was this trial:
his charitable grandmother bequeathed no chaos for her heirs.
He worried, would his mess be another's mare's nest?

He died, leaving an unkempt office and

orphans adopted,
the sick visited,
prisoners inspired,
homeless housed.

His grandmother smiled.

July 21, 2012

One Thing More

In my childhood family,
when we received a list of chores,
we were always annoyed to hear
that dreaded phrase, "Oh … one thing more."

So when I need help with late-life's list
on the way to that distant shore,
may my family not see me
as the annoying "one thing more."

June 10, 2020

Oyez

The crier strode down the street,
his gaze freezing the crowd.
He stepped up on a small box
and spoke in a voice quite loud:

Oyez ... oyez ... oyez!

The King decrees that by His grace,
we have been set free.

Both citizens and alien folk
have been set free.

This is true: both women and men
have been set free.

As His children, we can drop the yoke,
having been set free.

Gracefully adopted by the King,
through faith in His Son.
We're brothers and sisters of one another.
Now our search is done.

Believe your King!

Oyez! Oyez! Oyez!

This good news is for all.

June 29, 2017
Inspired by the book of Galatians

Picture This

Now whad'ya all go and do that for?

This here war is bad enough,
what with all the killin' 'n' fightin'.
No need to fake the picture
and pose my corpse.

Now I'm out of the blood and gore;
don't make no never mind to me no more,
'cept I don't want my mama seein' me here.
So keep the picture out of the papers, hear?

Aww, now whad'ya y'all go and do that for?

March 10, 2014
Inspired by a Civil War photograph
(http://www.usa-civil-war.com/GPhotos/g_den_orig.jpg)

Plague

(Exodus 10:21–23)

The first plague's like an occult trick
our priests could equal with magic sticks.
But the plague most troublesome we're dealt:
three days of darkness that could be felt.

April 11, 2020

Poinsettias

It stood there, silently,
along the Avenue of the Fountains,

a twenty-foot cone, large end down,

with red—
blood-red—
poinsettia plants
placed on the outside of the cone.

A sash of white poinsettias
came diagonally from the pointed top
across the blood tide,
angled like a mountain road
but with no switchbacks,

gently holding, staunching the red flood.

January 16, 2021

The Puzzle

He waved a no to
my offer of aid as
I reminded him the car door swings back.
I had dropped him off at the treatment center,
his wobbly, prideful gait steadied by a cane.

I saw him make it safely in,
then drove across the parking lot
to a spot where I left the car 'til
he returned from radiation.

Thirsty, I went to get a Coke, which—
seven quarters? (more than I wanted to pay, but hey)—
clunked and chunked and rattled
wending down the machine's labyrinth.

I walked to the waiting room
and entered, spied a jigsaw puzzle.
It was a thousand-piece seaside scene featuring
a lighthouse, sailboats, lobster traps.

The project magnetized my mind.
I grouped like items, though I'm
poor at doing it by shapes.
I did find some interlocking pieces.

My search for patterns went to
the straight sides for the picture edges,
some slack lines representing ropes,
bright objects not repeated elsewhere.

. . .

"Excuse me, your rider is here."
The soft voice rattled round my head.
A louder voice soon said, "He's ready,"
but puzzle fragments held me thralled.

I need more time. I curtly thought.
My work is not finished here.

Then a still and small voice intoned,
"Oh, but it is; others will finish this puzzle.
Now you go and do *your* job."

July 8, 2017

Read the Bible

It's important:
to watch your deeds,
to eliminate your greed,
to insure you live up to your creeds,
to be clear so you don't mislead.

Your attitude you must carefully heed

because

you may be the only Bible
some people ever read.

June 15, 2020
I read or heard the last two lines but do not recall where.

Salt

At the wake we wondered,
"Why had he been called 'Salt'?"
We had all known him but at different or brief times;
each of us had only one puzzle part.

The simple guesses, like an acronym
or what he put on his food, did not work.

"Well," said a childhood acquaintance,
"He was bullied and cried a lot;
he said he learned to like the taste of his tears."

His war buddy added, "His targets would be obliterated.
He wanted no foe or even friend to be able to use the blasted land."

A church member noted, "He brought out the best in people,
bringing to the task their strengths."

A cousin spoke up: "He saved our family traditions; no one else
was interested at first, but he persevered and preserved
the memories; now everyone is thankful."

His boss continued, "He always put in more than was needed;
he more than earned his salary."

Still, we did not understand why this man was called Salt.
No one image pinned him down.

November 28, 2014

The Sand Hand

He studied religions,
thinking, pondering

at great cost.

He walked the beach,
wondering, wandering,

exhausted.

He lifted the sand
in fisted hand

and lost it.

He lifted the sand
in open hand

and lost it.

He lifted the sand
in cupped hand,

smiled, and shared it
with the lost.

July 12, 2007

The Seam

As a flat, narrow, gently curved seam,
I wend my way 'tween sea and land.
I try to keep the two apart,
as I see the dispute is out of hand.

On one side, so-called cottages:
homes with golf-green lawns, long docks,
garages holding eight rare cars.
The other side has sea-drubbed rocks.

The windblown sands continually
cross me, blasting the palaces tall.
The homes drop rocks to staunch sea's flow
and end moon's tidal assault.

I provide a middling path for those
who cannot afford the homes so grand;
who can only walk the fine line
'twixt luxury and an ocean's land.

Grandparents bring their grandchildren
to see the ocean's ruinous plot,
the sea's relentless violence
and the houses' inner timber rot.

My efforts to reconcile the two
are, it seems to me, futile.

Yet

the Pole Star again appears,
and I resume my vigilant struggle.

May 28, 2014

Seven and Seven

On the occasion of my seventy-seventh birthday

Two sevens went out for a brisk walk,
sat together, and decided to talk.

They soon saw they were the same
and then decided to play a game

to see how many sevens-sightings
they could compile to their liking.

Seven brides for seven brothers:
did this please all the mothers?

Seven dwarfs helped Snow White;
it seemed to work out all right.

Seven Wonders of the World,
around which ancient travelers whirled,

sailing across the seven seas,
their sense of wonder they did please.

There are the seven deadly sins—
let's hope we're not caught therein.

A slot machine's jackpot is number seven,
but lucky players get out even.

Seven is a number most prime;
does this make it most sublime?

The sevens got up to go
and knew they would have to wait
a year to come around
and then be paired with an eight.

March 19, 2019

The Shadow

―•―

Clamped in my cramped condo, I sought relief in
a sunlit walk. My unzipped jacket was open to the
sun's rays that warmed both my body and spirit.

Back muscles tightened as I opened my
arms to receive God's bounty.

My face turned to the sun; impatiently, I opened
my eyes and saw the beauty I knew surrounded
me. My shadow was straight and solid.

But

off on the eastern horizon, a dark, dark cloud floated.

My head dropped to my chest;
my arms were limp at my side,
my waist bent and twisted,
my knees caved.

Downcast, I saw the shadow I cast and,
having forgotten my blessing-counting lessons,
was upset the shadow was crooked.

January 18, 2020
Thanks to Martin Luther for the germ of this idea

Shadows

The train slowly
wound through the desert.
The boy, looking out,
exhaled with a soft *wow*
his joy at his first Grand Canyon glimpse.

The thrown putty ball,
smaller than a marble,
struck his friend's eye,
swelling it to fearful size
before it shrank to normal.
Prayer and cure carried the joy.

The *Ode* played to the child
and again by the early teen,
who was surprised to find
the adults were right;
tears ran off his chin.

The young man making
his bride's hope chest
gouged the front and could only
with joy watch his grandfather
seal up that slip
with glue, skill, sawdust, and sweat.

*
**

Are these merely types and shadows
of the Joy that is,
that I know are
before us
and behind,
such sights, sins, sounds, and slips?

So can it be
we may only see
Joy's shadows far away
'til we humbly hear
the people's griefs today?

November 11, 2009

Shame

Blame became shame;
shame became my name.
That name made claim,
reframed my lame soul

until Christ's flame
reclaimed my soul.
Head games, stage names
dissolved,
and I could exclaim,
"My Lord!"

August 28, 2017

The Sheep

The ravenous sheep bleated, rousing the herder.
He grabbed his rifle and walked the perimeter
as he looked for signs of stalkers near the sheep.
He came up empty: no scat, no track, no fur.

He'd planned to move from the glade at dawn.
This old pasture, worn to stubble and dirt,
needed rest to shoot roots deeply, to grow thickly
and bring moisture up to the tips of each green blade.

Dogs guided the herd to the field
and reached higher ground above the pass.
In the sunlit pasture, dewdrops shone
from grass and spiderwebs, like cut glass.

Catching scent of a meal and water,
the sheep trotted to their reward,
their safe site, to avoid a slaughter—
Surely, the shepherd rightly led his wards.

The Shepherd

The shepherd was struck.
Distraught sheep bleat, scatter widely
'til they remember
Galilean green pastures
and await the shepherd's voice.

September 11

Sleep

The lunchroom was littered with chatter
from the time-pressed faculty.
There were ten minutes until the bell.

Through drooping eyes, he made a wager:
"I'll sleep and wake before the bell."
They laughed and took the bet.

He won, waking just before the knell,
not knowing his blood sugar sleep
was a summons from an earthly fell.

September 26, 2013

Small Plants

The small plants are dry
and tremble in the cold wind.
"Where are the gardeners?" they cry.
The small plants are dry.
Their plight comes with a sigh
as their dead leaves descend.
The small plants are dry
and tremble in the cold wind.

September 6, 2013

A Smile

His arms are folded on his desk;
the right hand cups the left elbow.
His chin rests upon his forearm;
his cheeks' creases parenthesize
the closed, broad U-shaped mouth.

February 6, 2016

Snow

The hurricane came, and then the snow.
Its fall was heavy, wet with slush.
My mission, laid upon me,
was to clear the clutter.
I was bone weary
but heard the voice
"Work well done"
at the
end.

November 8, 2012

The Song Goes On

Molly strains against the harness, pulls the plow
that jerks as Jim holds on to it.
The reins rest on his shoulders.
Boy and beast break the unworked ground,
worry the plain.

He guides Molly to keep moving straight:
sweat soaks his shirt, rivulets run down his back.
Ma said they must open this plot.
Near the field's border he swigs switchel
then slumps in fatigue.

Nearby, bees search blossoms.
One lumbers to the ground.
It struggles to lift itself
while a hive mate takes over,
gathers what it needs, and moves again.

The farm boy may take more rest now:
he lies down,
breathes deeply,
closes his eyes.
His brother calls his name as he crosses the field.
Jim waves a tired thumbs-up.
His brother furrows; the earth complains.
The larder will fill.

June 13, 2014

Spider Changing

The small spider went about his business.

He designed a web positioned just right
to catch the flying traffic in his net,
not so stiff that it would tear on contact,
with just enough anchors to hold it well.

He filled himself from what he harvested.

Over the summer, he noted changed days.
A colder sun rose later, set sooner.
Fewer flyers floundered in the web's embrace.

A new porch light now beaconed bug nightly.
Our sore, weakened designer moved his web
to meet the changing, chilling world.

June 28, 2012

Spit

(John 9: 1–12)

Spit spat
to the dirt
below,

made mud that,
on eyes rubbed,
sight bestows.

May 7, 2007

Still Tall

Standing tall, still shouldering cables,
like a giant erector set
with silent strength,
not knowing
(or at least not complaining)
that some condemn their route
as a landscape gash
and them as ugly,

carrying power
to cool my insulin,
to power my chair,
to light my emergency room,
and raise my cool pure water.

But let the lines fall
or even falter

so that

my computer flickers,
my stove stops,
or my team's play is missed,

I then futilely wish
the destruction of these
still tall
stoic servants.

November 25, 2008

Storm Damage

The winter storm split the tree nearly in the middle
and brought down a large section.

The logger gave us an estimate.

We decided to take the whole tree down.
We live in a very wooded section
of NH, with trees a dime a dozen.

It was a Wednesday when the workers came.
First the fallen trunk was limbed, and then
the remaining body was brought down.

But the saws' sounds could not still the images:
of Tolkien's last march of the Ents,
of youths' shaded laugh-filled picnic,
of a spring pool feeding tree roots,
of our dog rousting out small frogs.

These images emptied me,
leaving a regret-filled hole
with the loss and a wondering:

*Could I have saved this maimed life
that was sacrificed on the
altar of my convenience?*

July 10, 2012

Stumbling Block

When we set out the seas were fair;
few clouds in heaven blocked the sun.
The winds behind swelled our sails;
our hearts o'er flowed with mirth and fun.

The lookout saw a dark, dark cloud
scudding on horizon's rim.
He hollered to the deck below
a warning of a storm quite grim.

The captain in a harried tone
replied with anger in his voice,
"We must continue on, you swabs.
Our gold's below; we have no choice."

The rain closed in; the sails were torn,
yet we went on with yardarms cracked
until we foundered on the rock—
our gold the sea's rough surge hijacked.

"Abandon ship!" our captain cried.
We clambered out upon the Rock;
with storm's end we saw our Rock
could also be a building block.

February 10, 2020

Sunrise

My family went for a walk
before dawn to view
an Arizona desert sunrise.

We walked on the caliche;
the sound of boot-disturbed gravel
was the only noise we heard

as we trekked up a slope
in the pre-dawn light
to the ridge from where we'd watch.

At the top of the hill
the mountains to the east will
provide a perfect backdrop.

Only a few clouds
floated above the mountains
as we settled on chair-size rocks.

The sun rose slowly
but soon was so bright
all we dared look at
was the pale pastel
of the now pink clouds.

February 21, 2014

Temporary

Soft snow floats to earth,
cov'ring proud ways of summer.
Plows, sand, salt defile.

January 11, 2019

Thirty Days

"And what is so rare as a day in June?"
the poet asks of us.
There is an answer to that tune
we'll find with little fuss.

The childhood ditty of "Thirty Days"
can answer queries so.
It tells us that three other ways
do match our June's fine flow.

September, April, and November
each equal June's sweet show.
Forbid we fail to remember
Feb's rarest days in snow.

August 13, 2018

Thoughts on Coronavirus Days

Written during the pandemic of 2020

[expletives deleted]

?

July 5, 2020

Time Loved

He loved genealogy,
scrapbooks, family houses, stories,
relatives, and their final homes.

He tried to capture time,
to stuff that wind in a bottle
and cork it; to impale it
with pen to a sheet of paper.

But this wind had the winning wits,
as though it were alive
and more than the mere measurement
of movement.

The more he strove,
the more elusive it was—
like quicksilver.

The more he captured,
the less he kept—
like adolescents
too soon pushing love.

Not soon did he tire
of chasing this parade
that seemed endless,
but tire he finally did of this charade.

Then looking outside the time past
that was not his in the first place,
he made friends with eternity
at last.

July 6, 2011

Tree Friends

I heard the change in the wind
from whispers to whooshes
around the house's corners.
It bent bushes and scratched
tree branches against the window.

I had not checked the weather forecast
and now saw that winds—heavy winds,
hurricane-force winds—were expected.
They'll drive the sleet and snow horizontally.

Craa-ack! A branch breaking
like a rifle shot moved me from the window,
unable to know how close the sound.

Lightning blazed; thunder thudded. From the brief time
between the two, I knew the strikes were close.

The next day I went out to survey the damage.
I wore a heavy winter coat and my Wellington boots.
The woodlot was like a Narnian no-man's-land:
twisted trunks, iced splintered branches,
and trees uprooted with few unscathed.

"Hello, badger," I said as I came to his burrow
near an ice-coated oak.

"Hello, Rich. How are you?" he answered.

"How is the storm cleanup going for you?"

"Not well."
He pointed to a large branch
across his burrow door.
"Help me move it?"

"Sure.
How is it with the rest of the forest?"

"Poor," said badger. "I'm glad I have my oak."

"Let's go see the rest of our friends."

We looked at a tall fallen tree,
roots still clinging to the earth their fall raised.

It had had a full, proud, wind-catching crown.
Since its time as seedling, it had grown near the edge of a suburb,
far from protecting trees.

"See that, see that!" Badger pointed.
"Tall trees with prideful crowns crash more quickly."

We looked at another tree;
the buttress roots had been split
years before last night's stress.

Devastation and havoc continued to fill the view.
We came to a tree broken in the middle.
Its splintered spine revealed
a weakening years-old heartwood infection.

Farther on, we came to an area
where rocky shallow soil
was a place of poverty for trees,
providing no wealth for growth and health.

We passed lowly, flexible bushes that had survived.

Then back at badger's burrow,
we removed more debris.
I went home,
washed, went to town
to help my other uprooted, broken, frozen friends.

January 11, 2016

Trixie

Already two years have gone since Jean has passed,
when we inherited her shih tzu pet:
a bouncing clump whose flouncing black curls massed
around her tiny frame in ringlets set.

On the plane, my wife's foot, close to Trixie, did not relax
our dog. The shout, "Is that a rat?" disturbed our sleep
as Trixie made a break and then made tracks.
The passengers enjoyed her rapid leaps.

In Arizona, rugs kept Trixie's runs on rail,
but NH's bare floors proved slippery for her turns.
Each morning I could see only her tail
that flagged her bounces upstairs in four-feet churn.

So if you want no cute mutt,
a shih tzu's not the dog to grace your hut.

August 5, 2015

The View from My Office

I sit in my monk cell-sized office and
look out the window.
The green trees are about fifty yards away;
they're thirty, maybe forty feet tall.
Above them are the gray-streaked cumulus clouds
with the blue northern sky above that.
From inside I see, but do not hear, the trees sway.

Work weary, I stand to stretch and am now able to see
the old two-car garage droop where the west wall is gone,
the paint-peeled peak, and
the netless rusted hoop.
It used to be a good garage with
a now long-gone forty-foot shed to the left
that covered firewood and provided chicken roosts.

In mid-stretch, a movement catches my eye.
The black cat walks gingerly
through the grass, carefully lifting
each leg as it steps.
It abruptly moves its head;
something apparently caught its ear
or eye, as the cat did mine.

It stares and waits for something.
Its ears turn; its whiskers quiver:
a mouse perhaps?
A chipmunk morsel?
A bird unawares?
Gone is the smug indifferent manner; an intense stare replaces it
as the cat slowly crouches and creeps.

The cat is more patient, or is hungrier, than I.
I tire of watching the watcher and return
to my seat to stare and stalk:
a birdlike word,
a mousey phrase,
a chipmunk thought
upon which I can pounce, feast, but know
I too am being Watched.

August 23, 2013

Who Knew?

The bee flew by flowingly,
carrying life unknowingly.

April 11, 2020

Writer's Block

The mountains were encased in clouds;
the rain so slightly reached the ground.

The morning shower's pace picked up;
the shredded excess made rivulets
which ran to join eroding streams.

The valley's river ate all gifts
so placed, then ran on t'ward the sea.

The wealth of water broke the banks:
trees uprooted
fields flooded
relentless push of waste's fate sealed.

The deepening river slowed and swirled.
The narr'wing valley, the tree-choked channel
all blocked each drop from ocean's gate.

November 12, 2014

You Stress

On facing a blank page

This stress
is a distress.
But you can have
a stress of
eustress.

June 18, 2010

Printed in the United States
by Baker & Taylor Publisher Services